INTROVERT SUCCESS PROGRAM

HOW TO BE SUCCESSFUL IN BUSINESS AND CAREER

ANTON C. HUBER

Copyright © Anton C. Huber
All Rights Reserved.

ISBN 978-1-63957-111-6

This book has been published with all efforts taken to make the material error-free after the consent of the author. However, the author and the publisher do not assume and hereby disclaim any liability to any party for any loss, damage, or disruption caused by errors or omissions, whether such errors or omissions result from negligence, accident, or any other cause.

While every effort has been made to avoid any mistake or omission, this publication is being sold on the condition and understanding that neither the author nor the publishers or printers would be liable in any manner to any person by reason of any mistake or omission in this publication or for any action taken or omitted to be taken or advice rendered or accepted on the basis of this work. For any defect in printing or binding the publishers will be liable only to replace the defective copy by another copy of this work then available.

Contents

Acknowledgements   *v*

1. Business Culture And Introverts   1

2. Business For Introverts   6

3. Can Introverts Succeed In Business   9

4. How To Be An Introvert And Successful In Business   12

5. How To Succeed In Business If You Are An Introvert   15

Disclaimer   25

Acknowledgements

While the authors of this book have made reasonable efforts to ensure the accuracy and timeliness of the information contained herein, the author and publisher assume no liability with respect to loss or damage caused, or alleged to be caused, by any reliance on any information contained herein and disclaim any and all warranties, expressed or implied, as to the accuracy or reliability of said information. The authors make no representations or warranties with respect to the accuracy or completeness of the contents of this work and specifically disclaim all warranties. The advice and strategies contained herein may not be suitable for every situation. It is the complete responsibility of the reader to ensure they are adhering to all local, regional and national laws. This publication is designed to provide accurate and authoritative information in regard to the subject matter covered.

ONE

Business Culture and Introverts

Business culture is geared toward the go-getter, the team player, the networker, the entrepreneur and the leader. It's about power, getting ahead, cutthroat competition, deals and leverage. It is, isn't it? On the surface, this sounds like an automatic recipe for success for the extrovert and disaster for the introvert. But as you'll soon read, introverts can excel in this culture, by making the most of their unique attributes.

Since the early part of the 20th century along with the rise of corporations extroversion has been favored over introversion as a way of doing business.

Think about most job postings and resumes and the buzzwords you hear both from the job seeker's and the employer's perspectives: "work well with others; dynamic; driven; team player; shows initiative; strong leader; contributes ideas; outgoing and personable; sales-driven..."

While these are admirable traits, they are extrovert traits and they are not the only traits that are important in business.

The flip side of the coin is just as important - a strong work ethic and traits that ultimately lead to measurable results: "Conscientious; follows through; independent self-starter; self-motivated; persistent; focus on customer relations; trustworthy; curious; autonomous, self-directed, innovative, problem-solver, independent thinker…"

Introverted people have been perceived in a very negative light in the business culture mostly because of a false association of introversion with shyness. Even the dictionary definitions portray introverts as somehow socially flawed or inept. Introversion is perceived as a personality disorder: "Marked by interest in or preoccupation with oneself or one's own thoughts as opposed to others or the environment; shy or reserved." Definitions like these are written from the point of view of the extrovert, who sees the introvert's tendencies as negatives; something akin to saying that introverts are self-absorbed, self-centered social outcasts who don't care about anyone else, don't have any people skills and can't possibly succeed in anything except maybe basket weaving (that's if they can market their baskets). This is a very one-sided bias, but a very pervasive one. And what about the introvert who is thinking about flying solo and embracing entrepreneurship? Entrepreneurs in particular are thought of as highly extroverted people. Entrepreneurs rarely achieve success on their own and common knowledge says that this must be because the most successful entrepreneurs understand the power of networking and surrounding themselves with people who can help them. "Surrounding oneself with people" makes the introvert cringe and yet, there are many highly successful introverted entrepreneurs.

You've heard of Bill Gates and Warren Buffet? Introverts, wildly successful introverts and they are not alone: Steve Wozniak (co-founder of Apple, partnering with the highly extroverted Steve Jobs) and Larry Page (co-founder of Google) are introverts. Other notable introverts include former First Lady and women's rights champion Eleanor Roosevelt; civil rights activist Rosa Parks; the world's richest woman, Harry Potter author J.K. Rowling; and Albert Einstein.

What about the introvert on the way to the top of the corporate ladder? The irony is, as every CEO knows, "It's lonely at the top." And who would thrive better at that lonely pinnacle of achievement than an introvert? According to some estimates, 70% of CEOs describe themselves as introverts. How is that possible, when CEOs are also required to interact with people on a daily (sometimes 24/7) basis, speak in public, attend functions and meetings – heck, host many meetings and play the part of a gregarious, people-oriented leader... and schmooze to win clients and influence people?

You've probably heard, "it's not what you know but who you know" as a secret to success: putting yourself out there, being seen, striking up conversations, shamelessly promoting yourself and growing your list of contacts until you have one degree, not six, of separation between you and the rest of humanity.

If you're introverted, you probably feel a strong urge to hide right about now. That's not how you roll and you don't define success by the size of your address book. However, that gregarious, pushy business model is being forced down your throat. "Go out there, meet people, network..." Is it any wonder that introverts may feel hesitation when considering becoming business owners? Is it any wonder that the climb up the career ladder can be daunting to an introvert?

Like sexism, there is a strong bias toward valuing extroversion in the business culture. Business culture is still sexist and upholds sexist ideals: men are paid more and valued more than women and yet, despite the progress women have made, this bias is so deeply ingrained that it persists. Even women perpetuate the bias. It's the same with introversion. If a person grows up believing that introversion is a negative personality trait or worse, a psychological disorder, it will affect their success.

It's high time these biases are debunked! The old-school approach of valuing extroverts and dismissing introverts is faulty at best. To make the most of your business, or to thrive in your career, you will want to understand and employ the attributes of both styles of relating to the world. This applies both to yourself and to people you work with.

What might surprise you the most is that introverts are not a tiny minority. There are far more introverts among the general population than is readily apparent; in fact, most people are neither completely introverted nor completely extroverted. So for most of us, it's possible to take on traits that best serve our needs at the moment – for example, introverts can learn to make small talk and handle social situations; and extroverts can learn to value solitude to a point.

You can make a real splash in the business world if you're an introvert. No, no, that doesn't mean you'll necessarily be in the spotlight, it simply means that you have the same opportunities to succeed as any extrovert. It's all about learning to value and expand on your personality traits and attributes and use them to your best advantage.

TWO
BUSINESS FOR INTROVERTS

Lots of would-be entrepreneurs fail to get into business for themselves for one simple reason: they're introverts, and they're convinced you can't be both an introvert and an entrepreneur. But as a clear introvert with entrepreneurial aspirations, I'm here to tell you it just isn't so.

Here are things introverts should consider when they feel the entrepreneurial urge.

Being an introvert doesn't mean you are socially incapable. As I mentioned, I'm a clear introvert. I've been an actor, a speaker, and a salesperson in my lifetime, and I dare say I've been successful in each of those endeavors. But lest you assume I'm just a singularity, I assure you that many of the most successful actors, teachers, salespeople, and others who make their livings speaking to other people have been introverts. How did they do it? I guess the answer is different for each... but one common theme might be that entrepreneurial introverts are more in love with their Big Idea and their business than they are with their desire for "I-time." They realize that, sooner or later, to be a success in life you do have to interact with others; as introverts, they can find ways to do much of their communications either one-on-one or in writing, but they're not afraid of interactions with others. You know this to be true. Almost all introverts who are able to work for a living in ANY job will have to speak up at a meeting at least occasionally. So allow yourself to be a real introvert - other successful entrepreneurs have done it - but don't insist on a life of complete solitude if you want to make your business work.

An introverted entrepreneur should strike out on her own without going it alone. These days, there are many great home-based internet businesses you can get into, and the introvert is likely to be fooled into selecting an opportunity that seems completely solitary. The problem is that you have to learn the craft of internet business, and if you never interact with anything but that glowing rectangle in front of you, you won't get it. The best way to go about it is this: find a good community of entrepreneurs where you have colleagues committed to your success (I can recommend one), find a coach within your community with whom you can easily relate (we introverts greatly prefer one-on-one interactions to group discussions), and make sure the community provides top-notch training in making sales online. If you're looking for help getting started, I would be happy to take a shot at being your coach... give me a call, or (better yet) send me an email!

If you're not an excellent writer, work hard to improve your skill. Face it, if you don't want to reach out to your customers and colleagues in person or by phone, what are you left with? You don't have to be a Pulitzer winner or best-selling author, but you do have to learn how to get your message across quickly and cleanly in writing. I'm lucky enough to have had good journalism training as a plucky youth... but there are lots of good online writing courses out there, and taking one would not be the dumbest thing you ever did. Again, if you need coaching, find a good guide with whom you can relate.

Hopefully, those ideas might provide you with some inspiration... and inspiration will drive you more than introversion. I'll leave you with one more uplifting thought: I recently took an informal poll of some of the most successful people in my own entrepreneurial community, and I learned that, on average, they earn about two-thirds of their profits passively, through great investments and other wealth-building strategies... and only a third from direct marketing-type work. It was music to my ears! They don't spend all day and night on the phone or speaking to large groups.

As an introvert, and as someone planning to rise to the top in the internet business world, that might be music to your ears, too.

THREE

Can Introverts Succeed in Business

Organizations tend to celebrate and promote extroverted personalities, but by some calculations, introverts make up half of the population. That's an awful lot of talent to exclude from executive ranks.

Organizations tend to celebrate and promote such extroverted personalities, as opposed to introverts, who draw energy from ideas or one-on-one interactions. Such quiet types are often not as visible within companies, but by some calculations, introverts make up half of the population. That's an awful lot of talent to exclude from executive ranks.

It's the numerical equivalent of excluding women and similarly shortsighted. There's a bias in our culture against introversion. To use Betty Friedan's language from The Feminine Mystique, it's a problem in our culture that has no name pervasive, yet seldom discussed, at least until recently.

Certainly, introverts trying to make it in business face obstacles. As part of their hiring processes, some companies give personality tests that seem designed to weed out introverts.

If you survive that, you soon discover that Most of our workplaces are set up for maximum stimulation.

Companies have an inordinate belief in the power of meetings and brainstorming and they tend to promote people who make themselves visible, often by speaking up first (whether they have anything meaningful to contribute or not). As a result, "most of us, at a young age, learn how to act much more extroverted than we are.

But this ignores that introverts have several strengths that are helpful in business.

For starters, being inside one's own head a lot isn't a bad thing. We get our energy from what people refer to as our inner world.

Second, while introverts don't spend a lot of time talking, they do spend a lot of time listening, not a bad skill for managing client interactions.

Fortunately for introverts and the organizations that would like to tap their talent, technology is making it easier to be visible without shouting. What technology does, really, is it allows us to connect with other people in less stimulating ways.

Email introductions are infinitely easier for introverts than picking up the phone, and with the Internet, you can connect with hundreds, thousands, or millions of people without ever leaving the house. A white paper is easily shared and debated without having to fly somewhere to make a presentation.

And even rethinking meetings can help. Make sure to give people ways to contribute that aren't just to jump into the fray." Something as simple as handing out an agenda of a meeting in advance will give introverts time to think it through. And since introverts are often energized by such thinking, they'll probably have great ideas to contribute if you bother to listen.

FOUR

HOW TO BE AN INTROVERT AND SUCCESSFUL IN BUSINESS

I'm an introvert. But you say, "You're in PR. How can that be true?" I have successfully navigated my career as an introvert, but recently, it really struck home that being an introvert as an entrepreneur does have its constant challenges.

I've always been an introvert, and one of the biggest issues I've had to overcome is how to navigate being in an extroverted role without becoming overwhelmed by it.

The moment when it all changed

As an introvert having attention focused on you are challenging, and back in 2010 I decided to change a theme in my life I felt was holding me back.

There have been countless situations throughout my life which I ran away from because I had to stand in the spotlight, school head prefect, job promotions, speaking at conferences... so many, it was a theme in my life. And it was time to change it.

There was absolute silence as the audience waited. I looked out to the crowd, took a breath and I began to speak.

And do you know what happened? I realized that I deserved to be in the spotlight. I wanted people to hear me speak. I wanted a voice that would carry across the room into the hearts and minds of the audience.

Do you know why, because I had something to say? I had so many things to say.

What I had to say could change their businesses, could help them get more customers, build relationships with interesting people, help them build their profiles. What I had to say could do so many wonderful things for so many people.

It was the start of my journey to realizing being in the spotlight wasn't about me, it's about you the audience.

Turning the focus

I'm still an introvert. That has not changed. However I've learnt being in the spotlight as a recognized expert is much bigger than simply being in the spotlight.

I now know the more we share our ideas, opinions and expertise, the more we are making the world a better place.

I still challenge myself too. I find live TV scary! When I do live TV I think of the people watching. I think about how my expertise and knowledge is real. It's earned. And it needs to be shared because I have something to say.

Circuit breaker

The classic introvert gets energy not from other people, but by being alone. There are weeks where my energy will be zapped by hundreds of people. I love the adrenalin and the sharing, but I know I need to go sit on my rock.

I live near the ocean, and I have a rock that I sit on that connects me with nature and just distills my energy. It's the perfect circuit breaker.

Listening not talking

I've built my business through relationships. As an introvert, we are fantastic networkers and relationship builders.

Introverts are great at getting people talking (so we don't have to do the talking ourselves). This skill is also very effective in sales situations. Listening will get you many more sales than talking.

Ignoring the red notifications

Introverts are quiet people in a noisy world, and you can't get much noisier than social media. Social media is my bread and butter, and I love it.

But as the little red notification sign pops up on Facebook it means I'm getting zapped. It's useful to turn off social media sometimes, or at least acknowledge how it's impacting your energy and sense of self.

Taking the time to meditate

Mediation is all about introverting. The practice is about being in the moment and focusing on just one thing breath, mantra or even a candle flame. It's about removing distraction and allowing thoughts to come and go, but to not think at all.

FIVE

HOW TO SUCCEED IN BUSINESS IF YOU ARE AN INTROVERT

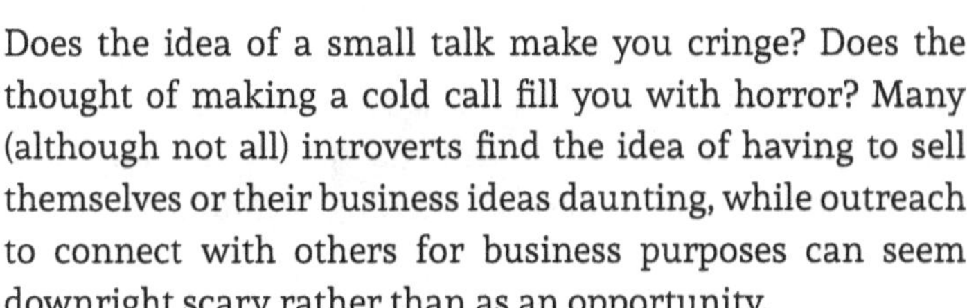

Does the idea of a small talk make you cringe? Does the thought of making a cold call fill you with horror? Many (although not all) introverts find the idea of having to sell themselves or their business ideas daunting, while outreach to connect with others for business purposes can seem downright scary rather than as an opportunity.

This doesn't mean that introverts can't be successful in business indeed; many successful CEOs through to salespeople are introverts. The key to success isn't always about being able to be the most outgoing person in fact, quite a lot of extroverts tend to get tangled up in believing that all talk and bluff is good, when it can actually wear out clients and scare off customers.

Don't fight your nature. Constantly forcing your-self to mingle, chit-chat and cold-call will take its toll. Doing things that you hate on a regular basis is a surefire recipe for burnout. All that stress can take years off your life! Don't try to be someone you're not. Instead, try to develop the business model that fits the real you; learn to be comfortable with who you truly are. And most importantly, believe that you're as capable as any other person at succeeding in business for an introvert; belief is everything because you don't like to present a dishonest or embellished front, and so if you believe that you can do it, you are already on your way.

- Although each person is individual and expressions of introversion vary in both type and intensity, common traits of the introvert include a tendency to think before speaking or acting (sometimes seen as slow to act), able to make good eye contact when listening, less so when talking, softer when talking and may appear to be hesitating or hunting for words, need frequent solitude to rejuvenate as too much socializing can drain their energy, feel stronger when in a one-to-one situation over group situations and tend to prefer a few close confidants/friends over befriending everyone.

Focus on your strengths. Sometimes there is a tendency to suggest that introvert qualities are inappropriate for business wheeling and dealing. Detractors might suggest that being quiet, slow to sell oneself and unwilling to party on are not helpful for sealing deals and convincing customers. This is shortsighted and undermines the aspects of being introverted that can actually make an enormous difference to business. For example, being good with one-to-one discussions is a definite advantage when convincing individual clients and others because they are made to feel special, totally focused upon and treated as an equal. This cannot always be said for a more forceful approach to selling that doesn't let up and tends to keep pounding away at the client some clients (perhaps introverted themselves) can be repelled by an all-talk, never ending spiel about the benefits and wonders of a product or service that barely lets them think or get a word in edgewise. It's therefore important to identify your strengths and be able to apply them to your planned business tactics. Here are pluses for your personality type in business:

- You appear calm and composed rather than hyper and evangelistic in pursuit of the sale, the goal, the teamwork, etc. In-your-face, pushy and over-excitable selling is now a thing of the past, as consumers have become far savvier and has higher expectations of building trust and mutual relationships that they can rely on should things not go according to plan.
- You're less likely to approach a deal as having to happen *right now*, giving clients or peers time to consider and think through what they'd like. It might surprise you but less pressure can often bring a client to agree instead of not going through with a deal, precisely because they were given space.
- You're likely to be great at building trust, mutual agreement and a sense of respect through your listening skills and your desire to ensure that the customer, partner or other relevant business person is on the same wavelength as you and will return the respect.

- You're less likely to feel a need to sound right all of the time or to put words/thoughts into the other person's mouth or mind. This is because you understand and respect the need for space and thinking time. Indeed, you are likely to be very good at picking up body language clues showing a person shutting down or glazing over more than an extrovert can (or wants to), and adjust your approach accordingly.
- You respect the questions asked of you. While extroverts can be brilliant at explaining things and emphasizing benefits, they can also oversell and create a false sense of just how good a deal it really is, out of over-enthusiasm and a desire to keep things really positive all of the time. An introvert is more likely to listen, to analyze the concerns of the other person and seek ways to solve the problems raised by customer's questions rather than brushing them aside with platitudes.
- You, far more than an extrovert, will connect with the introvert customer. This means that you'll listen carefully, acknowledge concerns, give space and be prepared to let the person walk. An introvert customer is far more likely to come back, even months later, because they will remember your consideration for their feelings, needs and interests and the fact that you didn't brush them off.

Find the right business. Jumping from one business opportunity to another and quitting everything you start does this sound familiar? People fall into this trap because they get excited about the profit potential but fail in doing the work involved. When evaluating potential businesses, ask yourself: "Will I really be able to do the work involved in the business?" In other words, choose a business that you believe in, passionately. No matter what the motivation for your belief, it has to be there, so that you can throw yourself into it heart and soul, with total conviction. That way, you get to stay totally honest and free of having to worry about embellishing the business' virtues and benefits because you're already totally sold on them. For an introvert, this sense of personal belief is vital to success in business and must not be overlooked. It doesn't mean you have to love or even like every aspect of your business (see the next step for getting the right help) but it does mean that the underlying reason for going into this business is what drives you and has meaning for you.

- Pursuing business opportunities that you absolutely love will show in your ability to connect with others. An introvert who is doing what they believe in and are passionately driven by tends to be happy talking about it. In fact, it can be hard to stop an introvert in this situation from talking too much! This added confidence can help you to open up more when socializing and networking.

Don't go it alone. Nobody is an island and nobody can be a master or mistress of all trades. You can try but you'll be worn out and worn down in no time. Hire the right people, the best people, to do those aspects of the business that just aren't you. This begins by being honest with yourself about what you are good at and about what you're no good at doing. It's not a judgment that weakens you it's just the opposite because by getting a strong team in to cover those things you don't like doing or can't do, you become stronger and are freed up to concentrate on doing what you do best. Nobody expects one person to be brilliant at accounting, legal work, sales, marketing, advertising, service provision, design, writing, speaking, and running conferences, and so on. Pick your fortes and then find your team to cover the other aspects. At the beginning a business, good financial and legal advice can be purchased by the hour and is worth every dollar it costs you.

- While your tendency as an introvert may be to research it to death all yourself, don't let this lull you into thinking you've got it all covered. Practical experience is something that takes time and you are best getting the help of others to help you learn processes and to better understand consequences as a novice business owner, manager or participant.
- Try to get an even balance between extroverts and introverts in your team. Too many like people and you'll all agree with one another until inertia; too many different people and you'll risk spending all day clashing.
- Outsource direct selling and cold calls. You can and probably should hire other people to do any direct selling that you find overwhelming. Even if you're on a budget, you can still get "commissions-only" salespeople who get paid a percentage of sales, which means no upfront cost to you. However, do the interviewing of these people for yourself so that you're satisfied they are who you want as part of your team. Secondly, go back to the step about strengths and be sure that you're not neglecting those sales where you might be best at the helm, the times when your one-to-one connection will really make a difference.

Be pragmatic rather than hung up on perfection or being real all of the time. Pragmatism allows the introvert to be an actor, to rehearse before social events, business meetings and sales and marketing moments. Forewarned is prepared, so the pragmatic introvert is wise to do their homework about each upcoming social situation, learning names, likely topics for discussion and knowing the product or service that they need to pitch/sell/promote/inspire others about in total detail. You don't need to deviate from believing in what you're doing but the pragmatism does require some suspension of concerns that you're doing something that isn't as true to yourself as you'd like. Everyone has to step into personas professionally and it isn't about lying—it's about putting forth the best self for that occasion, about making others feel comfortable and about letting your business shine rather than seeming lackluster. This does require effort but then so do most things when running a business. A pragmatic introvert will do at least the following:

- Study the background, motivations and interests of clients, competitors and peers. Don't ever be caught off guard; homework done will be repaid tenfold.
- Study before big events, business meetings, conferences, and any other schmoozing occasions so that you know who is attending, where they come from and what they're likely to want from you. Don't go in blind no business person ever should but even more so when you're trying to protect your introvert nature from being overwhelmed.
- Network. While this thought may make the introvert quake, networking is really about making the right contacts and staying in touch with them. And you can

do this one-to-one, even outside of actual networking events and you can stay in touch by email. Really, it is that simple but it is so important!

- Avoid conflict. You probably already do but how you avoid it matters. You can avoid conflict and still get your passion across by one of several methods. One way is to simply be patient and listen to everyone else, then to speak out, drawing in all that you've heard beforehand and to seek compromises that work for all. Another way is to evade the conflict; this simply means constantly monitoring the risks through listening, watching and noting subtle changes of demeanor and manners and either changing tact if you're in charge or removing yourself if it's a group issue about to blow up.

Turn challenging situations into an issue of tact, diplomacy and manners instead of a battle of good versus evil or honesty versus dishonesty. Introverts tend to have a strong sense of justice and a strong desire to be honest, sometimes to the point of being blunt and too real. Clearly, being too frank can be plain rude at times and being undiplomatic can destroy your reputation and possibly also that of your business. If you feel that your principles are challenged or that people are beating around the bush instead of getting to the point, seek the ethical higher ground of resorting to good manners and being diplomatic, with practice, you can be tactfully forthright and people will still respect that you're not compromising without feeling like you've bull-doze-red them into noticing reality.

Plan smart. There are ways around having to spend an entire day or night around people, even in a business context. As a professional, it doesn't hurt to let people know that your time is valuable and that you can make social events for a short time but that you have "other pressing engagements" (even if it's just feeding your cat and curling up by the fire in relief at having quiet time by yourself). And even when you can't get away, such as at big conferences and the like, plan to slip out for a refreshing walk during a break or simply take five minutes to regain your composure in the fresh air outside. In your own workplace environment, try to carve out a corner for yourself, even if you can't manage your own office. If you own or manage the business, work elsewhere some of the time, like from home or use travel time to dictate notes, etc.

- At conferences and seminars, it never hurts to turn up to morning tea or lunch slightly later when at a conference (you'll avoid the queues for the buffet anyway) and then slipping away earlier than everyone else, explaining you need to get your papers/affairs in order. Also, people understand the need to network at most business occasions and this can be used as an excuse to get away momentarily or when you're starting to feel overwhelmed.
- Make the most of the time you do spend networking to ensure key people have your business card before slipping away and be sure to follow up with an email. Actually do follow up so few people do this that you'll be remembered and a good relationship can be built up from here by way of emails and online networking.

Use online networking to the maximum. The Internet allows people to find the right business contacts and skip the usual schmoozing. You can network with people through discussion forums, social networking websites like Twitter and Facebook, or simply by sending an e-mail to introduce yourself. Using the electronic contact is easy, efficient and not intimidating. It's also considered the norm in current times, and nobody thinks any the worse of you for using these methods in fact, it's now expected!

Market on the Internet: Even people who hate selling can succeed in Internet marketing. Your website does all the selling so you don't have to. Orders are placed on the website without your intervention, and customer service is done via e-mail. The Internet is truly an introvert's dream!

- If you're great with design, words and layout, you might be able to do a lot of this aspect yourself. However, it still doesn't hurt to get help to ensure that you're on the right track

Disclaimer

Introduction

By using this book, you accept this disclaimer in full.

No advice

The book contains information. The information is not advice and should not be treated as such.

No representations or warranties

To the maximum extent permitted by applicable law and subject to section below, we exclude all representations, warranties, undertakings and guarantees relating to the book.

Without prejudice to the generality of the foregoing paragraph, we do not represent, warrant, undertake or guarantee:

- that the information in the book is correct, accurate, complete or non-misleading.

- that the use of the guidance in the book will lead to any particular outcome or result.

Limitations and exclusions of liability

The limitations and exclusions of liability set out in this section and elsewhere in this disclaimer: are subject to section 6 below; and govern all liabilities arising under the disclaimer or in relation to the book, including liabilities arising in contract, in tort (including negligence) and for breach of statutory duty.

We will not be liable to you in respect of any losses arising out of any event or events beyond our reasonable control.

We will not be liable to you in respect of any business losses, including without limitation loss of or damage to profits, income, revenue, use, production, anticipated savings, business, contracts, commercial opportunities or goodwill.

We will not be liable to you in respect of any loss or corruption of any data, database or software.

We will not be liable to you in respect of any special, indirect or consequential loss or damage.

Exceptions

Nothing in this disclaimer shall: limit or exclude our liability for death or personal injury resulting from negligence; limit or exclude our liability for fraud or fraudulent misrepresentation; limit any of our liabilities in any way that is not permitted under applicable law; or exclude any of our liabilities that may not be excluded under applicable law.

Severability

If a section of this disclaimer is determined by any court or other competent authority to be unlawful and/or unenforceable, the other sections of this disclaimer continue in effect.

If any unlawful and/or unenforceable section would be lawful or enforceable if part of it were deleted, that part will be deemed to be deleted, and the rest of the section will continue in effect.

Law and jurisdiction

This disclaimer will be governed by and construed in accordance with Swiss law, and any disputes relating to this disclaimer will be subject to the exclusive jurisdiction of the courts of Switzerland.

www.ingramcontent.com/pod-product-compliance
Lightning Source LLC
Chambersburg PA
CBHW051405250726

48656CB00006B/2281